THE WORLD IS UPSIDE DOWN

A MEMOIR OF A CHILD OF HOLOCAUST SURVIVORS

THE WORLD IS UPSIDE DOWN

A MEMOIR OF A CHILD OF HOLOCAUST SURVIVORS

Livia Birnbaum Rothman

I dedicate this memoir to the loving memory of my remarkable parents, grandparents and all the victims and survivors of the Holocaust as well as of other genocides. 'Never Again' is not just an expression, it is a commitment to spread the message of the Holocaust time and time again all over the world until all people get the message that discrimination, prejudice, bullying and violence are not acceptable and never will be against any human being because of race, religion, national origin, sexual preference or any other reason!

To my precious children Erica and Steve and to my incredible grandchildren as well as to all my future descendants: I wrote this memoir with you in mind. Know and don't ever forget who you are and where you came from!

I am forever grateful to my husband, Joel, who has been lovingly supportive of me and my parents through the years, and always understood the importance of retelling my family's story. Also, he has been the editor of this memoir and helped me with corrections and suggestions. Thank you!

Jason, my wonderful son-in-law, thank you for reading this memoir and giving your input and always being supportive.

Erica and Steve, your input about this memoir has been very important and very special to me.

Praise for *The World is Upside Down*

"Livia's unique and detail oriented narrative deeply delves into the details of World War Two, the Holocaust, living under Communist Rule, the challenges of being a teenage-immigrant and more. Indeed, Livia's unique narrative speaks volumes of the challenging yet unique life of being a Child of Holocaust Survivors."

–Ruth Isaacs-Holzer

Ruth Isaacs-Holzer is a teacher/substitute teacher in South Bend Indiana, and a daughter of a mother who was a Child Survivor of the Holocaust from Vienna, Austria. Her mother was in an Internment Camp for political prisoners in Kazakhstan because her family had German papers. She is a member of the Governing Board of the 'World Federation of Jewish Child Survivors of the Holocaust & Descendants.' She is also a member of the 'SlidingDors' organization of the Jewish Federation for Children of Holocaust Survivors as well as various Facebook groups related to the Second Generation and the Holocaust.

"The writing style made me feel as though the author, Livia Birnbaum Rothman, was composing the book as she lived it; i.e., each section appears to me to have been written contemporaneously. Obviously, her memory of the interconnectivity and experiences of her many family members, friends, and herself is quite amazing - not to mention colorful as well.

In the earlier pages, I felt the challenges of just trying to survive when she was tracing her parents, their family and others connected to them before and especially during the war years when they suffered so much. Later in the book, I laughed a lot and was quite jealous of her ability to maintain frequent communications with even far-away relatives.

It is the stories of her family's lives and then her personal experiences that got me! How I wish I had the ability to remember so much about my family, and in such detail.

its writing allowed me to really feel the author's pains as she was adjusting to life in America while learning the language. Her sense of humor shined there and everywhere. Truly, upside down!

Also, the author's love for our freedoms here in America was very moving to me. She had lots to compare that to, from before she left Communist post-war Hungary. That's amazing in itself, given that she left there at the young age of 15!"

—Mindelle & Ira Pierce

Mindelle Pierce is the author of 'Love With No Tomorrow; Tales of Romance During the Holocaust.' She has dedicated over fifteen years of her career to studying and teaching the history of the Holocaust. As a child of Holocaust survivors herself, she has a personal connection and insight into this history.

Ira Pierce, P.E. P.C.; Engineers, Architects, Environmental Scientists. Ira assisted Mindelle with the collection of facts and information for the above book and acted as editor and IT advisor.

About the Author

Livia Birnbaum Rothman spent the first 15 years of her life in Hungary as an only child to two Holocaust survivor parents. In 1963 she moved, together with her parents, to the United States. She lives in New York with her husband close to her two children and two grandchildren. She enjoys spending time with her family and friends and devotes some of her time to Holocaust Education.

Disclaimer

This book is a memoir. No events have been fabricated. It is based on the recollections of my parents' experiences, my experiences, documents, artifacts and photos given to me by my parents and members of my family.

Table of Contents

Prologue

I was born in Putnok, Hungary in 1948 to two Hungarian Jewish Holocaust survivors; only a few short years after the end of World War II. Putnok is a small town in Northern Hungary, near the border of Slovakia in a mountainous region. The tragedy that befell my parents and their parents was unspeakable, but they raised me with the hope that I would have a good life.

In 2010, when I retired from my job after 36 years with the New York State Office of Disability Determinations, I made a commitment to devote some of my time to Holocaust Education, and to tell my parents' stories. I became involved with the Kupferberg Holocaust Resource Center at Queensboro Community College. While I spent time there, I had the opportunity to read many Holocaust stories of survivors. After a time I received docent training at the Museum of Jewish Heritage in Manhattan. In my search for a second-generation group (children of Holocaust survivors) I joined a group that was affiliated with the Holocaust Memorial and Tolerance Center in Glen Cove, New York. Through this group I was introduced to the many programs and exhibits that this museum has. I also met an incredible group of people who were employees and volunteers at this museum. They became interested in my family's story and encouraged me to put together a presentation for students and adults who visit the museum and for those, outside the museum, who are interested in the Holocaust. With the help of staff and volunteers, we put together a PowerPoint presentation for my family's story, including text, pictures and videos. Since 2013 I have been talking to live audiences as well as videoconferencing with thousands of people. I am forever grateful to the Holocaust Memorial and Tolerance Center in Glen Cove for opening the doors for me to tell my story, for educating thousands of people about the Holocaust and about intolerance. It never occurred to me that I should write a memoir, but now I decided that I wanted to put, not only my parents' experiences as survivors, but also my experiences as second generation and as a child who was raised in Communist Hungary and subsequently immigrated to the United States, into words in the form of a memoir.

My Mother

My heart is sobbing
My tears are flowing
Today I think back about this year
Although I am already over everything
        Olga Jelinek, Allendorf, bomb factory, 1944

Valeria (Vali) Kaufmann Birnbaum was born in Jolsva (Jelsava), Hungary (now Slovakia) on January 14, 1918. She was the 5th of 6 children with two older sisters, Margo and Klara, two older brothers, Ernő and Sándor (Sanyi aka Alex) and a younger brother, Dönci (Edmund, Ödön). Her father was a businessman who owned a textile/dry goods store. My mother spoke Hungarian, Slovak, and German and knew how to play the piano and the accordion. She spent some of her time teaching young children how to play the piano when she lived in Jolsva. Life in her small town was quiet until the start of

World War II. However after the war started her brothers were called up to serve in the Hungarian Army as forced laborers (munkaszolgálat) with other Jewish soldiers. Her younger brother, Dönci (Edmund aka Ödön) was sent to the Russian front and he was murdered there. He was only 22 years old at the time. In spite of the Jewish laws that came out and restricted Jewish families in major ways it was still relatively quiet in Jolsva until the German Nazi occupation of Hungary on March 19, 1944. Shortly after the occupation the Hungarian Jews were rounded up and moved out of their homes into ghettos and then to concentration camps. When my son, Steve, was in Middle School and the class was studying World War II, he wanted to tell my mother's story and experiences during this period to his class. We lived in New York City and she lived in Cleveland, Ohio, so my mother decided to write a letter to my son describing what happened to her and to her family after the occupation. She wrote the following:

We lived in Jolsva, a town which was located at the border of Hungary and Czechoslovakia. Jolsva was part of Hungary at that time. My family in Jolsva included my parents, myself, 5 children, and my brothers' wives. Two of the 5 children belonged to my sister, Klara and her husband. My sister and her husband lived in Slovakia, which was occupied by the Germans in 1942. They sent their 2 children to my parents because they believed that the children would be safer there. Jolsva was part of Hungary at that time, and the Hungarian Jews were not being deported until 1944. Up until the last minute everyone hoped and foolishly believed that the Hungarian Jews would not be touched.

On May 10th, 1944, my family and I were taken to a ghetto in Pelsoc (Plesivec), also at the border of Hungary and Slovakia. We lived there with other Jews until June. On June 10th we were transported to a town near Miskolc, Hungary, and spent the night in a brick factory, sleeping on the ground. The next morning they pushed us into a cattle wagon, about 80 people into a very small compartment, and we traveled like that for three days. We had no food and no drinks; we were starved and thirsty. We arrived in Auschwitz 'at the conclusion of this trip.

My two brothers were in forced labor with the Hungarian Army. I also was spared. Dr. Mengele did the selection. At the time of the selection I was helping to carry one of the children. He said to me, 'Is that your child?' I don't know why he asked, and I did not know then what impact my answer would have. I told him the truth. I did not have any children then and none of the children were mine. He said, 'Give the child to its mother!' I did that, still not knowing the implications. At that point he told me to go to the right, and told all the rest, including all the children, my sisters in law and my parents, to go to the left side. The girl I was holding was Marika (young daughter of my brother Ernő).

We had to remove all of our clothes and our bodies were shaved all over. The next morning when I woke up, I went outside to look for my parents, but I could not find them; I sat down on the ground and started to cry. An SS (German Nazi soldier) came over to me and asked why I was crying; he told me that my parents and all the rest of my family were killed in the gas chambers. I was in Auschwitz for close to three months. I was starved and life was a torture. There was a Polish Kapo in charge of our group. I had a friend from Jolsva who was in my group; Bözsi (Elizabeth). Bözsi was a seamstress, therefore, she was allowed to stay in the barracks to sew. The rest of us had to get up at 3:00 AM and leave the barracks; we could not return until 9:00 PM. We were standing outside or sitting on the ground. The SS came several times a day to do roll call (count). Everyone had to be present at roll call because if anyone were to be absent, they would kill the entire group.

One day Bözsi gave me hot water through an opening in the wall. It was 'their' idea of soup: hot water with some kind of margarine. Right at that moment the whistle sounded to indicate that we had to run out for roll call. I was so hungry that I drank down the hot 'soup,' in a flash, and burned my throat, mouth, and lips. When I woke up in the morning my throat, mouth and lips were full of blisters, and I could not swallow. Bözsi looked at me and said,

'If the SS see you, they will take you to the gas chambers.' For the next three days I hid among dead bodies so nobody would see me until the blisters healed. Bözsi found another woman from another barrack to take my place during roll call. This woman was a doctor from Miskolc, Hungary. She tried to help people. It was a miracle that none of us were caught and killed.

At the end of my stay in Auschwitz we had another selection in front of Dr. Mengele. We had to march in front of him naked, and he selected the women who were still strong enough to go to work. They took our shoes and replaced them with shoes that had wooden soles. They transported us to Allendorf by train. Allendorf is located at the German-French border. We got our new assignments to work at an underground bomb factory. We had to leave our barracks every morning at 6:00 AM and walk an hour and a half to the factory.

My work at the factory involved climbing on top of the third bomb. The bombs were arranged in order on top of each other. I had to attach the bomb to something that carried it into the next room, where they filled it up with poison. It was difficult to step on top of the bombs because there was very small space for my feet, so I could not do my work with those wooden shoes. I had to remove my shoes and do my work barefoot. I worked like this all winter long in this cold environment. I had no stockings or pantyhose under my dress.

In January I became ill with dysentery. I lay in bed for four weeks. I don't know how, but I got well. There were no doctors, no medicine. At the end of the illness they sent me back to work, but I was very weak, so two weeks later I developed a throat infection with high fever. Again I recovered. By this time rumor had it that the Americans were getting close to the French-German border (the Liberation Army).

On March 23rd, in the evening, we lined up and walked all night long.

In the morning we stopped in a field, and lay down in amongst some hay. The following evening we were told to continue walking, but I could not continue. I told my friend Bözsi that I am not going. She told me that they will shoot me, but I did not care anymore. Another woman from Miskolc, Hungary, whose name was Magda, also decided to stay with me. The group was told to get up and leave. The SS woman yelled 'Hauptsarfuhrer.' There were others who could not march either and did not get up. The SS knew that the American Liberating Army was near and they did not do anything to us; they just left us there.

We walked into a small lake and waited until the rest of the group marched off. When it was all quiet, we returned to the field. There were eight of us left. We stayed in the field for three days; starving and exhausted. On the third day we saw a white flag in the nearby village. One of the girls went to the village to find the American soldiers. Two soldiers came for us with a car; they transported us to the village, and placed us in German houses. We were in this village for three months, and we were fed and taken care of. At first everyone was sick, but slowly we all recovered.

I traveled from this German village to Prague, Czechoslovakia by bus. The trip took three days. We were in Prague for a week and from there I travelled to Pozsony, (also in Czechoslovakia) by train to meet my brother, Alex (Sanyi), and we went to his deceased wife's aunt. (Alex lost his wife and two children in Auschwitz.) Then, I went to Eperjes to meet my sister, Margo. I, then, also had to face my sister Klara and her husband, to recount the tragedy of what happened to their two beautiful children in Auschwitz; the children whom they tried to save by sending them over the border to stay with my parents in the Hungarian section of Slovakia.

I learned to live with the memory of these horrors, but I could never forget nor could I ever get over what they had done to me, to my family, to *my friends and to all the Jews of Europe. I survived because I was young and strong, unmarried, without children, had friends who helped me out and also, I survived because I was very lucky. In 1947, I got married and moved to Hungary. In 1963, my husband my daughter and I immigrated to the United States to reunite with my sisters who immigrated before us.*

While my mother was staying in the German village to recover from the atrocities and illnesses that she suffered there was an American soldier who had an accordion. My mother knew how to play the piano, and also was able to play that American accordion. She played it so well that the soldier gave it to her as a gift. When my mother left the village to go back to reunite with her family, she carried that accordion together with her repatriation documents. Those were the only two belongings that she had in the world. She played that accordion for her family and friends for many years until she was forced to part with it.

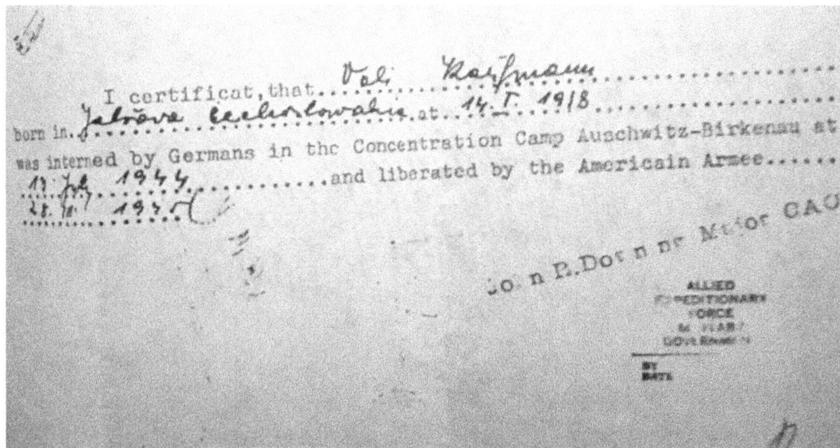

I certificat, that....*Vali Kaufmann*............
born in..*Jalšava Cechoslowakia*..at..*14. I. 1918*..........
was interned by Germans in the Concentration Camp Auschwitz-Birkenau at
17. III. 1944............and liberated by the Americain Armee......
28. IV. 1945

Jo n R.Dorn nr Major CAO

ALLIED
EXPEDITIONARY
FORCE
MILITARY
GOVERNMENT
———
BY
DATE

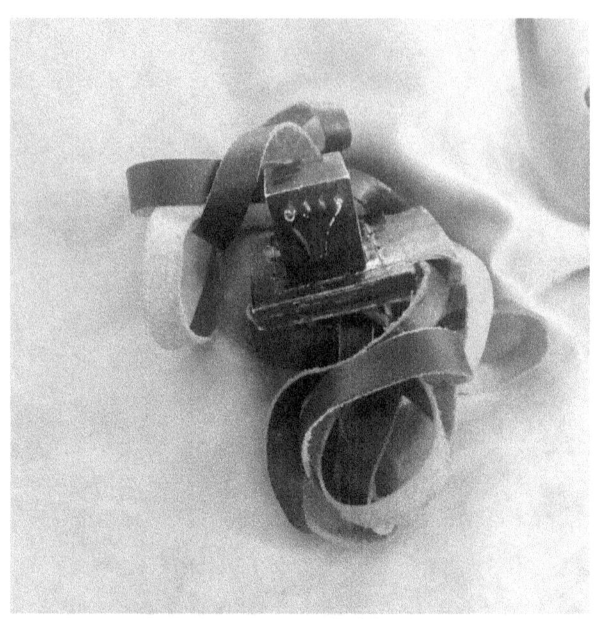

My father's Tefillin and bag.

My Father

I lie here, like a beast covered with vermin as the fleas resume
their seige with renewed vigor. But mercifully
the army of flies has retreated as darkness falls, and my
captivity and life are both shortened by a day.
Miklós Radnóti, Seventh Eclogue, Forced Labor, 1944

My father, Louis (Lajos, Lali) Birnbaum was born on May 18th, 1910 in Putnok, Hungary. He had two brothers, Hugó and Sándor (Sanyi aka Alex) and one sister, Elza. His father owned a shoe store and he worked in that shoe store with his father. My father spoke Hungarian, Yiddish and German. He attended Yeshiva, and he was a very observant religious man. I knew him to be very serious, but he also had a very strong sense of humor with a cutting edge. He was frequently joking around even with people he didn't know. His brother Hugó was also extremely funny. Life in Putnok was quiet, as it was in Jolsva, before the beginning of World War II, although Anti-Jewish laws went into effect there also. After the war started the Hungarian government started calling up Hungarian Jewish men to forced labor (Munkaszolgálat) with the Hungarian Army. My father was in forced labor with the Hungarian Army from 1941 to 1944. These Jewish men were involved with marching ahead of the Hungarian and German Armies and preparing the front lines for battle. They were not armed, so they could not defend themselves. Also, their work was arduous hard labor which involved building bridges, roadways and digging ditches and shooting trenches. Food and water were scarce and treatment was very harsh. Many did not survive; that's how my mother's younger brother died. My father escaped from forced labor in 1944 and was hiding until he was liberated by Soviet Russian soldiers. Although at first, he was a prisoner of war, when they found out that he was Jewish they let him go. He returned to Putnok to look for his family. He found out that his father and sister, Elza with her family, were also murdered in Auschwitz. His mother passed away before the war. His two brothers were also in forced labor with the Hungarian Army and returned. They both settled in Budapest (the capital of Hungary).

There were many forms of resistance during the Holocaust and one of them was spiritual resistance. As I stated before my father was a deeply religious man, so when he was called up for forced labor with the Hungarian Army, he took a religious object with him: a tefillin. The tefillin is a box like object that has small prayers inside it. People put it on their head and it has leather straps that people can strap around their arm. Jewish men were not allowed to practice their religion while in forced labor or have any religious objects. My father took the tefillin into the outhouse and prayed there every day until one day he heard some noises and thought that he would get caught and get killed, so he was forced to get rid of the tefillin. What my father did was very risky, but he took a chance because religion meant so much to him. After the war he continued to practice his religion even under Communism.

My father made a statement in Hungarian under oath which was signed by a Notary Public on March 25th, 1966 in Cleveland. I translated it into English:

Putnok

*Putnok was a peaceful farming community on a fertile plain
in Northeastern Hungary, between the river Sajo and the
Carpathian mountains. The soil was rich, the air and water
were clean and the climate was harsh in every season.*
Eva Brown, If You Save One Life

What was life like for a little Jewish girl in Putnok, Hungary, whose
parents just had unimaginable losses and liveda in torturous situations
during World War II? While I am trying to reach back in my memory, it's
very difficult to remember all the details. My father was quiet and busy
with working in a shoe store. He got a position as manager in a store that
once belonged to his family but was no longer his because the government
repossessed it. You see, Hungary was liberated by the Russian troops
of the Soviet Union and was now under Communism/Socialism. Private
property and private businesses were forbidden. I was too young to know
or understand anything about this. I knew that I had a mother who loved
me very much but was often sad and cried. She spent time looking at
pictures of family members who, I found out, were dead. I slowly found
out how they died and looked at those pictures with her. The pictures
included my maternal grandparents, Ethel and Eugene, my aunts Irén
and Elza with their children, Marika, Robbie, Tommy, and my aunt Klara's

children, Vera and Adi. Those beautiful faces are etched in my memory and will never be forgotten. My mother was always busy in the kitchen cooking and baking delicious food and pastries. My father and I loved her food. To this day I can never replicate her cooking and baking and amazing skills in the kitchen.

We had no blood relatives in Putnok, but we had a family of Holocaust survivors, whose children were my friends. We spent a lot of time together in each other's houses; eating, singing, playing musical instruments. My mother played the piano and the accordion. Life in Putnok seemed quiet and peaceful, as far as I can remember; although my father fell ill a couple of times with a collapsed lung. He was a smoker from age 10 to age 60. He ended up in a hospital in Budapest to treat his lung condition. When my mother accompanied him to Budapest, I stayed with our close family friends, the Guttmans. They had two children, Bandika and Editke. Bandika was about my age, and we played together, but he was also very rambunctious. He once got a hold of a pin and stuck me with it. I was never seriously hurt, but I learned to protect myself. All the children went to Sunday School/Hebrew School together at the Szamet family's house. Szamet bácsi (Mr. Szamet) frequently chased Bandika around the table because he was misbehaving there too. Nevertheless, we, children had fun together. These memories remind me how we supported each other, and how deep the connections were between us. Now Bandika is in Israel, the Szamet family is in Brooklyn and I am in Queens.

In Putnok we didn't have indoor plumbing, we had an outhouse, but I used a potty inside the house. There was a grand piano in my house, which my mother often played, and I too was learning how to play the piano on it. The first and only song I can remember playing was 'Boci Boci Tarka' (a children's song), which I now sing to my grandchildren.

They also listen to this song on YouTube frequently.

Our neighbor in Putnok had a little boy named Lacika, who was around my age. We played together frequently. When we were about 5 years old, I ran off to the neighbor's house to play with Lacika. My mother didn't notice that I left, and I didn't think to tell her. When she realized that I wasn't home she was looking for me and couldn't find me. Then I finally came home and saw that my mother was very upset and angry because she couldn't find me. I was punished with the 'fakanál!' That is a wooden spoon that many Hungarian parents used to spank/ discipline their children. That was the one and only time that she used it on me in my entire life. My mother was not an abusive person. Now I know that more than anything, she was frightened that something terrible happened to me. Of course, looking back on her history, that was perfectly understandable. I have felt that fear and panic too when I thought my children could be in danger. Is it a normal reaction of a mother whose child is suddenly missing, or was it an overreaction of a traumatized individual who suffered so much personal loss? Did my mother have Post Traumatic Stress Disorder, which was then inherited by her daughter also?

Me (Livia) in Putnok. School picture in elementary school.

The Hungarian Revolution of 1956

Although Antisemitism was not a central issue during the revolution, dozens of anti-Jewish atrocities took place. According to Andras Kovacs, Antisemitism was kept under the carpet from 1948 to 1956, but when the government lost its control in 1956 personal and collective anti-Jewish violence was unleashed.

Laszlo Molnar, Antisemitism in Hungary

An 8-year-old girl was standing with her mother on the main street of her small town, and together with a large number of towns people, they were watching tanks with soldiers driving through with a morose expression on their faces. The look on the soldiers' faces mirrored that they didn't seem to like what they were doing, but they were forging ahead anyway. While there was no fighting in the town, the soldiers knew that they were headed to armed conflict where their lives will be in danger. They also knew that the people on the other side of the conflict were in infinitely more danger because the Soviet Russian soldiers were in larger numbers and far better equipped than their Hungarian counterparts [freedom fighters] in Budapest, the capital of Hungary. Yes, the tanks were heading to Budapest. The soldiers were wearing khaki uniforms with coats, looking ahead and focusing on the road. They didn't pay attention to the people on the side lines, just kept moving. They came from he Soviet Union [Russia], through Czechoslovakia, into Northern Hungary; into my little town, Putnok, and I was the 8-year old girl. They didn't stop, didn't talk to anyone and didn't even look around, just kept going straight ahead in the direction of Budapest. You see that's where the fighting was, and that's where the Hungarian Revolution of 1956 took place against Communism and Soviet occupation. Clearly the revolution was squashed. Was that good or bad or neither? It depends on who you were and what was your perspective.

The reason for the revolution was understandable. The Hungarian people were oppressed under a one-party system, Communism, and were occupied by Soviet Russia; there was no freedom and no democracy. There was no free speech, no free enterprise, and you couldn't own property or businesses. If you tried to speak against the government, you were thrown in prison and you were tortured or killed. There were spies everywhere. The system was more invasive than our internet. People were afraid to talk on the streets and on public transportation. You saw very quiet people on the trains; minding their own business, not even looking at each other. It was a way of life and you became accustomed to it. There was also a lot of poverty and food and housing shortages with long lines at the grocery stores and several families sharing apartments. So, people became tired and fed up with this way of life; especially in the capital, Budapest, where conditions were even worse than in the countryside. Young and brave high school and university students united, organized and decided to start an armed revolution against the occupying troops of the Soviet Union. They were outnumbered in every way. The help that they expected from the 'West,' including the United States, didn't come. The politics were complicated. If the 'West' would have come forward to help a small armed group of revolutionaries, they would have compromised their very shaky relationship with a superpower, the Soviet Union, during the cold war. So, the Hungarian freedom fighters were on their own, and were handily squashed by the Soviet Russian troops. There were many unfortunate casualties. However, at least, Communism in Hungary after the Revolution was weakened. A new leader was appointed and a 'gulyás' (combined) Communism – Socialism became the form of government. This new government still didn't allow any freedoms, private property or private business. People continued to live in fear.

My father and our family lived in fear for several reasons. Some people didn't know, and some people didn't want to admit, but the Revolution was hijacked by the Hungarian Nazis, the Arrow Cross (Nyilasok). This group was extremely antisemitic and was strongly proactive during World War II on the side of the German Nazis. They literally killed thousands of Jews during the Holocaust. They fought in the revolution against the Communists, but they also renewed their preoccupation with Jew hatred and pursuing their plans to murder Jews. We were still living in Putnok when, during the revolution, my father came home with flyers in his hands. My mother and I looked at him waiting to hear what happened. I still have a picture in my mind of my 8-year-old self looking up at my father and seeing fear in his eyes. It was scary! He held up a flyer and showed it to us. It read, 'First we will take care of the Communists and then we will go after the Jews.' He told us that these flyers were being dropped from a helicopter, clearly by the Hungarian Arrow Cross. I remember him saying: 'They know where we live! We have to leave!' We packed up and left Putnok and moved to Budapest, into my uncle Hugó's apartment. We left all our furniture and our beautiful grand piano. Our friends, who were our Holocaust survivor family, all followed us to Budapest for the same reason. Uncle Hugo and his family crossed the border to Austria during the revolution and emigrated to Israel. No matter which side we were on during the revolution at that time in Hungary we were hated and persecuted. I can say with confidence that if the revolution would have been successful against the Soviet Union, we Jews would have had to run for our lives. Eventually we left the country anyway. Thousands escaped during the revolution and many continued to leave after the revolution continuously.

Budapest

Budapest is a beautiful city! We lived there from December of 1956 to November of 1963, possibly during my most formative years (8 to 15). We as a family, and I as an individual had many unique experiences there; some were challenging, and some were very pleasant. We lived in the center of the 7th district, which was known as the old Jewish quarter (at the time I didn't know it). During Communism people weren't supposed to practice any religion. However, as I mentioned before after the revolution ended the new government was a combined Communist-Socialist government that was more lenient than the pre-revolution government. My family and I did practice Judaism; especially after 1956.

The apartment we lived in was a one-bedroom apartment, with a living room, dining area, kitchen and a split bathroom (the toilet was in a separate room from the bathtub and sink). There was no central heating, and we had a ceramic fireplace in the living room. The bathroom was cold because the heat didn't reach there. During winters my mother collected hot water in a basin, and we washed in the living room near the fireplace. The kitchen warmed up from all the cooking. There was a lot of that taking place, since my mother was always cooking. We had no washing machine, dryer or refrigerator, and no television. There was a radio which we used to listen to Communist news, music, and soap operas (The Szabó Family). The bedroom had a large bed, some drawers and an old crib. The living room had a small bed, a large wall unit with books and pictures on it and a dinette table. I slept in the living room. My bed was across from the wall unit. The wall unit displayed pictures of my maternal grandparents (Esther and Eugene), my aunt Klara's children (Vera and Adi), my aunt Elza and her two sons (Robbie and Tommy), and my uncle Edmund (Dönci). Uncle Edmund was murdered on the Russian front, while he was in forced labor with the Hungarian Army during World War II, and the rest of the family on those pictures were sent to the gas chambers of Auschwitz. These were the pictures that my mother showed me time and time again since I was born. I have had these faces in my head since I was born. Every night after my parents went to sleep, I lay on my bed across the wall unit in the living room where these pictures were displayed. I couldn't sleep. I knew that these people were dead, and I knew how they died. Each night the pictures got bigger and bigger like ghosts, but I never told my parents. I knew how much my parents suffered and how much they lost. I was very protective of them from a very young age and never wanted to hurt them. So, I looked at these pictures night after night and I was scared, but I kept it to myself. The faces of those beautiful people remain etched in my mind for as long as I will live. I am no longer afraid of these pictures of my precious relatives, but instead I proudly display them in my house and show them to the world (through a PowerPoint presentation). I want the world to know that these people existed and were murdered simply because they were Jewish.

Cleveland, Ohio. When I turned 18 years old, I had rhinoplasty by a plastic surgeon that my mother found through talking to her survivor friends. My mother was remarkable and gave me strength to face my life with all its challenges.

As I mentioned before, after the revolution the government became somewhat more flexible regarding the rules of Communism/Socialism. While we were still living under a one-party system with very limited freedom and no private property, my family was able to practice Judaism. My father became the Rabbi's assistant at the Kazinczy Street Orthodox Synagogue, and he held this job from 1957 to 1963. I visited this synagogue again in 2006 after its most recent renovation. The interior of the synagogue is in Turkish motif, and it is breath taking. It was not yet open to the public, but I explained to the caretaker that my father worked there, and he let me look around inside.

Back in the 1960's we observed Sabbath and all the Jewish holidays and kept a kosher household. My mother koshered the chickens at home in salt water, but I played a very significant part in shopping for chickens. When I was in my early teens my mother used to send me to the market (piac) to purchase live chicken. After I bought the chicken, I walked with this live chicken to Mr. Szamet's house, who was the shochet (kosher slaughterer). He slaughtered the chicken, pulled the feathers, wrapped it up and gave it back to me to take it home. This was an experience that will stay with me for the rest of my life because he did all this right in front of me, not even considering that I might be shaken by this experience. At home my mother soaked the chicken in salt water to make sure it was kosher and made delicious chicken soup or chicken paprikash from it, and I still ate it. I could never resist my mother's cooking. Every Friday night we ate cold carp with jell (kocsonya). That carp spent some time swimming in our bathtub before it was beheaded by my parents and prepared for dinner.

We bought live chicken and live carp, but thankfully not live cow. Beef came from the kosher butcher, that did also exist in Budapest.

Life in Budapest had its ups and downs. Every Sunday we went to Margaret Island (Margit Sziget) by boat on the river Danube. Margaret Island was beautiful, full of trees, grass, flowers, fountains and spas. We never went to the spas, but we walked around, sat on benches and admired the beauty of the island during spring, summer and fall. The neighborhood where we lived was within walking distance to the opera, operetta, and other theatres. The theatre district was Budapest's Broadway. My family and I attended the opera and operetta on occasion. I loved the operetta so much that I even went by myself if no one was available to go with me. There I saw 'The Merry Widow,' 'The Czardas Queen,' and many other shows with famous Hungarian actors, actresses and comedians. The comedians were mostly Jewish and extremely funny. Comedy was my father's favorite. He and his brother, Hugó, both had a very good sense of humor and often liked to joke around. Unfortunately, I didn't get to know Hugó because he was already in Israel when we lived in Budapest. My father had another brother in Budapest, Sándor, but he and Sándor often had disagreements and didn't spend much time together. Sándor was self-employed (maszek). He owned a very small private shoe repair, which was allowed by the Hungarian government, but he was under constant scrutiny, was often accused of breaking the law and was imprisoned. He remained in Hungary after we left. I corresponded with him for a while until he passed away. Someday I plan to visit his grave in Budapest.

Even at that young age when I lived there, I saw crime in Budapest. I used to sit on my balcony and watch drunken men staggering every day. There was a great deal of alcoholism. An older single woman lived in my building. One day I heard my parents talk about the fact that she was ill, and she was addicted to opium. That's when I learned about drug addiction for the first time. In school, when I was 14 years old, I found out that the girl who told me that I couldn't play with her because I was Jewish was admitted to the hospital. Later we found out that she was pregnant and was having an abortion. We also found out that she was sexually abused by her father. I felt so sorry for her that I decided to visit her in the hospital. I never saw her again after that because she never came back to our school. In one incident, I was coming home from a walk, and when I opened the door to my building, I noticed that a man was behind me exposing himself to me. I got scared, ran up the stairs so fast, and I never looked back. Many people were poor, many had to share space with other families, many turned to alcohol and drugs and some unfortunately turned to crime.

My family's experiences with Socialized Medicine were extensive. We had national healthcare for all in Communist/Socialist Hungary. Patients had to go to a clinic and couldn't choose their own doctors; a doctor had to be assigned to you. I had teenage acne for which I was unsuccessfully treated. Once my skin became infected after a medical procedure in the clinic, and I had to take antibiotics. Again, I was unsuccessfully treated for an underbite. I am still experiencing problems with jaw pain because of that. When we needed serious medical treatment, such as surgery, we went to a doctor of our choosing privately and paid him 'under the table.' My mother had a hysterectomy that way and I had an appendectomy by the same doctor. This was technically against the law, but it was done on a regular basis. When I arrived in Cleveland, Ohio, at the age of 15, I went to the dentist. He looked at my mouth and said, 'Your mouth is full of cavities. Didn't they have dentists in Hungary?!' There were dentists in Hungary in the 1960's, but dental care was inferior there at that time. I do believe their health and dental care have improved since then.

When I was 11 years old, I became ill with flu like symptoms, fever and a rash. My parents called a pediatrician, who made a house call. Again, this was done privately and against the strict regulations of Socialized Medicine. The doctor sent me for a chest X-ray, and we found out that I had Tuberculosis. To my parents' dismay I had to go to a Sanitorium for children with TB. The pediatrician arranged this admission for me. The Sanitorium was in the mountains of Buda, but we lived in Pest, on the other side of the Danube. I was with children about my age. The children on the unit I was placed in were making fun of me because they found out that I was Jewish. My mother came to visit me every weekend, and I immediately told her what was happening because I was very unhappy. She spoke to our pediatrician, who was also Jewish. He arranged for me to be transferred to another unit and spoke to the staff. The children on the new unit were friendly, and I learned to live with this situation for three months. The medical treatment there was excellent, we also had school and performed chores. We spent a lot of time outside in the fresh air. After three months I went home with restrictions on my physical activities (no gym) and medications that I had to take for 12 months (PAS and streptomycin). I was completely cured with no lingering illness or any further issues. When I returned to school at home, I needed a tutor to catch up, but only in Math.

Sanitorium in Buda; last row, 1st from R: me (Livia) with a group of girls who were patients.

Camp in Buda: I am in the 2nd row, 2nd from the Right.

The Sanitorium was not the only place I spent time in while I was in Buda. I was in the beautiful mountains of Buda many times between 1957 and 1963. My parents rented a cabin in the mountains during the summer and we spent our weekends there. I also went to a Jewish summer camp, which, amazingly, existed in Buda. I had a very good time in the camp. We put on shows, we went swimming and did a lot of other fun activities. When I wasn't in camp, I also spent time in our cabin with my friend Panni. She and I attempted to make meals for ourselves while we were there. One summer I was able to go camping with a group of girls from school at Lake Balaton. Hungary doesn't have an ocean or a sea, but it has rivers and a very large lake. Lake Balaton is great for swimming, fishing, wildlife, camping, and resorts and spas. My parents and my teacher allowed me to join the 'Young Pioneers.' Strictly speaking it was technically a 'Communist/Socialist' youth organization, but the only reason I wanted to join was because I was interested in traveling to new places with my school mates. Most of the other teenagers were there for the same reason. These were good times in Hungary, but shortly after this experience my family left Hungary to come to the United States. My parents wanted something more for me and wanted to reunite with our family in Cleveland.

One of the highlights of my life in Hungary was receiving packages on a regular basis from Margo in America. Everyone, including my friends, neighbors, teachers and classmates, knew about the goodies that came in those packages. Margo was my aunt, my mother's sister, who lived in Cleveland, Ohio since 1949. The packages started arriving when I was a little girl in Putnok. While I am sitting here writing, I clearly remember a talking doll that came in one of the packages. That doll was one of my favorite toys for a while. After we moved to Budapest, and as I got older, I learned to appreciate some of the other items that came in those packages. They included dresses, pants, shirts, bathing suits, and more sophisticated toys. I wore some of those dresses in Budapest. Some of the items, such as bathing suits, that didn't fit me or my mother, we sold or gave away. People were begging to buy them. I had a Russian language teacher; she was a young attractive woman, and she always bought bathing suits. Fashion in Budapest was behind other Western nations. Stores didn't carry new fashionable items. Also, people had limited income, but they would rather spend the money on clothing that came from the West than what was available in Hungary, even in Budapest, in those days. One of my hobbies was to collect paper napkins of different styles and colors. Margo sent me different paper napkins of all types, which I definitely couldn't get a hold of in Hungary. I also got paper dolls and paper clothing for them. I loved dressing those paper dolls. Lots of family pictures came from Margo as well; pictures of my cousins, Vera and Joe, pictures of Margo and Irving (her husband), pictures of Vera and Paul (Vera's husband), and later, pictures of Vera and her children. I heard many stories from my mother about Margo and her family, and I got to know them through pictures also. In addition, my mother also had another sister, Klara and two brothers, Ernő and Sanyi. Ernő lived in Czechoslovakia with his family and Sanyi, with his family lived in Israel. Klara, Adolf and Ivan lived in Israel for a while, but then moved to Cleveland in 1956. My mother told me stories about all of them, she corresponded with them on a regular basis, and we received lots of pictures. My extended family lived far away, but I always felt very close to them. The love between them and us was obvious even across the miles.

Ernö, his wife, Ica, and his daughter Eva (my cousin) lived in Pelsoc (Plesivec), Czechoslovakia, very close to Putnok, just on the other side of the border. They were relatively close to Budapest also. They frequently visited us, and especially loved spending time in Budapest. When I was about 14 years old, I visited them in Plesivec by myself. My parents didn't like to travel. Eva and I were born in the same year only a few months apart. Uncle Ernő was a very loving and affectionate person, and everybody who knew him loved him. While I was there, I was complaining of stomach pain. I remember him treating me with tea and charcoal pills (szén pirula). He was very attentive to me since I was a guest, and Eva and I were competing for his attention. Eva had a very close relationship with both her mother and her father. She now lives in Minneapolis and I live in New York, but we have been in contact very frequently by phone, computer and in person

In Budapest: wearing a dress that I (Livia) received in a
package from Aunt Margo; very early 1960's.

when possible. Ernő and Ica are gone now but they live on in my heart and my mind with the rest of my very close-knit extended family who passed.

My father's brother, Sanyi lived in Budapest, but had no wife or children, and we had no other family in Hungary. My parents entertained the idea of leaving Hungary just like many friends and family left before them. If they would go, they would go to Cleveland, Ohio, where both Aunt Margo and Aunt Klara lived with their families after 1956. Why would they leave?! They would leave to escape Socialism/Communism, they would leave to give me a better life and more opportunities, they would want to rejoin my aunts, uncles, and my cousins in Cleveland. They would go to Cleveland, Ohio and not to Israel because life was easier there. Aunt Klara and her family left Israel for that reason and moved to Cleveland. I was in my early teens and I was neutral about leaving the country. I wasn't familiar with any other lifestyle. I would be content wherever we live as long as I am with my parents. My parents were torn because they feared a new life in a new country and a new language. With the anticipation that we would eventually leave they hired an English tutor for me to study English. I learned English grammar but didn't really learn to speak. So,

In Minneapolis: from R to L: me (Livia), Joel, my cousin (Eva); on my lap: Steve; on Joel's lap: Erica; and Eva's children on her lap.

my parents applied for a visa from the United States government and for a Hungarian passport. Interestingly enough we received the passport fast, but not the visa. The quota for Hungarian immigration was filled in the United States because of the 1956 revolution, and the large number of Hungarians that came into the United States at that time. So, we waited and waited and finally received the visa and permission to enter the United States. However, my parents were still vacillating. I remember going to the government office to pick up the papers, filling them out, returning them to the government office, and then revoking them more than once. I remember thinking it doesn't matter to me where I live as long as we are together, but I wished that my parents would make a final decision and stick with it. The visa was about to expire when my parents suddenly decided that we must leave. They quickly invited my Uncle Sanyi (my father's brother) for a farewell dinner. We quickly threw together a suitcase of clothing, pictures, religious objects and other important items and my mother's infamous accordion, which she never wanted to part with. However, we didn't have time to get permission from the Hungarian government to take the accordion out of the country, and we didn't get permission to take more than one suitcase worth of items. We got on a train to Austria and eventually to Trieste, Italy with a suitcase full of pictures, some clothes, an American accordion, which would finally be returning to America. In addition, my mother took a lemon and a knife (which she hid) with her. My mother made lemonade for us all the time, wherever we lived. The lemon and knife made it to Customs in New York, but we had to say good bye to it there. The accordion unfortunately never made it past the Hungary – Austria border. The Hungarian border patrol confiscated it and took it away from us, so the American accordion never made it home again. My mother missed that accordion and what it meant to her (liberation by the United States Armed Forces in 1945). When we arrived in Trieste by train, we boarded an Italian ship, Vulcania, and started our 17day voyage to the United States of America.

The MS Vulcania

The Italian line was founded in 1937 through the merger of the Genoa based Navigozione Generale Italiana (NGI), the Turin-based Lloyd Sabaudo and the Trieste-based Cosulich STN lines, encouraged by the Italian Government. The new company acquired the Cosulich-owned ships MS Saturnia and MS Vulcania.

Michael L. Grace, History of the Italian Line
and the MS Vulcania

Early November of 1963 we boarded the 1,760 passenger ocean liner, MS Vulcania in Trieste, Italy, near the border of Yugoslavia. The passage from Trieste to New York was expected to last 14 days, but it turned into a 17-day voyage. The Vulcania was a beautiful ship with fancy decorations, furnishings and good Italian food. If we were on a vacation, we would have been able to enjoy it, and some people did. Most of the passengers were immigrating to Canada and the United States, and many seemingly had a very pleasant time on most of the trip. The ship stopped in Venice, Naples, Barcelona, Gibraltar, Lisbon, Halifax and New York. Many passengers got off and spent time in these various locales, but my parents and I didn't feel like we were on vacation. By the way, when we came to Lisbon, there was an announcement on the intercom that Jewish passengers should not get off the ship because the Portuguese government is antisemitic and

nnot be trusted. So we stayed on the ship all the way to New York, but we
d go on the deck and enjoyed the fresh ocean air of the Mediterranean
d the Atlantic oceans. The dining room was very large and beautifully
corated, the food was good, but much of it was foreign to me because it
as Italian food. I was first introduced to pizza on this ship, and I didn't
ke it; I thought it tasted like cough medicine. It seems very funny now
cause next to Hungarian food Italian is my favorite, and it includes
zza. I eventually learned how to make pizza in school when I took home
onomics in Cleveland. I really enjoyed the meals on the ship and they
rved wine with dinner every day. I was nearly 16 years old at the time,
ut no one was concerned with my age, and I was served wine. In Budapest
used to drink wine on Friday nights for Shabbat. My parents didn't
revent me from drinking it on the ship either. However, after a few days
discovered that I was getting headaches, and we thought that maybe
could be from the wine. When I stopped drinking it the headaches
topped. Fortunately, I don't get headaches from wine any more.

The trip was proceeding uneventfully until we crossed into the
tlantic during the second week of November. My parents and I didn't
xperience any sea sickness. However, one day the ship became very
nstable. We were 3rd class passengers and our cabin was at the bottom
f the ship. The waves were very high and covered our portholes. In
act, the water started coming into the ship from the bottom, and there
vas water everywhere. People were getting sick to their stomachs and
omiting all over the ship. Most of the passengers were Italian, and they
vere screaming in Italian. The only phrase I caught was 'Mamma Mia.' My
ather, being an observant Jew, put on his tefillin and tallit and prayed
rom his siddur (Jewish prayer book) for hours. My mother was upset and
scared. The Italian maintenance crew who was working tirelessly to plug
up the holes and the leak in the ship thought that the situation was funny,
and they were laughing endlessly. I must have thought that everything
will be all right when I saw them laughing because I continued walking

around the ship and going to the dining room. I was one of the very few people who didn't get seasick. I was also one of the very few people who went to the dining room and ate meals. When I got to the dining room the waiters were sitting and relaxing while they were waiting to see if any of the passengers came for meals. I ate my meals by myself at my table. I walked out on the deck and many people were sitting on the floor sick. How did I walk around on an unstable ship that moved from side to side so much that we were practically upside down!? There were large wooden poles inside and I ran from pole to pole as I grabbed hold of them. Miraculously I never fell, and I never got sick. After a few days of this chaos the storm came to an end, the leaks were fixed, the ship stabilized and we continued on our voyage. Shortly after this incident we arrived in Halifax, Canada. This was my first but not last visit to the beautiful city o Halifax. Believe it or not I was on a cruise from New York to Halifax twice since then. On my last trip I visited the Maritime Museum of Canada, where I found information on the MS Vulcania, but unfortunately the passenger list from November of 1963 was destroyed in a fire. Our last stop on the Vulcania's voyage was New York City. The ship pulled into New York Harbor on November 22nd, 1963. We went through customs, where they discovered that my mother had a lemon and a knife and she was asked to give that up. We were then met by people from United HIAS (Hebrew Immigrant Aid Society) and were transported to Idlewild Airport (now John F. Kennedy Airport). We boarded a flight to Cleveland, Ohio, and the flight was uneventful. This was my first airplane ride.

Cleveland

We arrived in Cleveland on November 22nd, 1963 in the early afternoon. We were met by my mother's sisters, Margo and Klara. The three sisters didn't see each other since about 1948. The reunion was very emotional with lots of hugging, kissing, laughing and talking. Those three always found something to talk about and never stopped talking until the day they all passed. They are most definitely talking right now in a special place in heaven. A most wonderful and challenging chapter in our lives started that day.

The five of us boarded a bus that would take us to Cleveland Heights, which is where my aunts lived and we were going to live. We continued the talking and laughing when someone turned to my two aunts and asked, 'why are you so happy?! President Kennedy was killed.' Total silence and shock took over. President Kennedy was dead?! Even I knew about President John F. Kennedy, the young American president that the whole world loved. People on the ship asked me where we were going, and when I answered 'to America,' they said, 'oh you are going to President Kennedy.' Everyone thought we were so lucky. How did it feel to arrive as a new immigrant in a country where their president was just assassinated?! What kind of country is this?! These questions were going through my mind. With all these thoughts and feelings of shock and uncertainty we arrived at Aunt Margo's house in Cleveland Heights. It was a very nice house with lovely furnishings, a front lawn and a backyard. She and her husband, Irving owned this house. That was a new concept for me because in Hungary nobody owned property. What really impressed me though was that there was a large family waiting for us: Uncle Irving (Margo's husband), Uncle Adolf (Klara's husband), my cousins, Vera, Joe, Ivan, Aunt Zsenka (Irving's sister), Paul (Vera's husband), and Vera's (and Paul's) three children, Grace, Cheryl and Steven. From having one bachelor uncle in Budapest, whom I rarely saw, I now had a large extended family with aunts, uncles, and cousins, and they were so happy to see us. The love within this extended family was unparalleled and continued until most of them passed and the rest of us moved to various parts of the country. To this day we still talk, send pictures, attend occasions and visit each other when possible. Due to a current pandemic in this country and in the world some of those visits had to be cancelled, but will have been rescheduled by the time you read this memoir.

The Immigrant Experience

*They come here starting from scratch in search of job security or
education that will help them on their feet. Native-born Americans
should know more about the full story of our immigrant experience.
Know that we are not different because of where we come from, but
rather we all seek a better life and equal opportunities that lead to
happiness and peace.*

> Araceli Hernandez, What Every American Should Know
> About the Immigrant Experience

United HIAS and the Jewish Family Services (under the auspices of
the Jewish Federation) rented an apartment for our family and furnished
it with old, but intact and usable furniture. We even had a small black
and white television and a toaster. We also had a refrigerator and central
heating; all of which amazed me. I was so excited with all the technology
that we didn't have in Budapest that I wrote about it to my friend, Panni.
She wrote back, 'who needs a toaster when you can toast your bread
in a pan on the stove.' Maybe it sounded like I was bragging, but it was
really my way of expressing my amazement at the advanced technology
compared to what we had at that time in Hungary. I loved the television,
but I didn't understand anything that was going on. I listened to radio
also. I figured out even without understanding the language that when

there is a program on either radio or on television, they break into the program with something that has nothing to do with the program, but I didn't understand why. Imagine someone trying to understand the program without knowing the language and then they change the subject. Later, when I asked one of my cousins, he told me that these are commercials and advertisements for products that companies try to sell. What did I know about free enterprise and capitalism?! To me it sounded confusing, but I quickly picked up on it. As I was learning the language, I also lamented the fact that these radio and television personalities spoke too fast. By the time I figured out a word I totally lost them. While I was in 9th grade in Budapest, I now found myself in 8th grade due to the lack of English language knowledge. I was placed in ESL (English as a Second Language), art, cooking, and social studies and math. I liked art and I did well there, I learned to make pizza in cooking, but I didn't want to eat it, and I didn't understand anything that was going on in Social Studies. In math they were studying algebra, which was old hat for me because I knew it all from school in Hungary, and I was bored. ESL was a very important class because many of the students were from different countries and spoke different languages. Although there were some Hungarian speaking students, the teacher didn't allow us to speak our native language, and we all spoke to each other in English. Socially this was the most important class for me because this is where I made friends in my new country. We all lived in Cleveland Heights very close to each other, and it just so happened that most of us were Jewish. My new friends were from Poland, Romania, Israel and Hungary. I eventually met a very good friend from Yugoslavia who was not Jewish; she was one of my best friends. She passed away from breast cancer at age 65; may she Rest in Peace!

I was immersed into the English language from all sides: from school, from TV/radio, from ESL and from socializing with all my new friends and communicating in English. I picked up the language quickly, but with a heavy accent. Many people still didn't understand me when I was talking and often misunderstood me. Needless to say, I didn't understand or actually misunderstood people; even teachers in school. Sometimes I handed in the wrong assignment even years later due to a misunderstanding. I wrote a paper for my English teacher about what it's like to be misunderstood or not be understood and conversely misunderstand and not understand. She was very impressed with my content and had me read it to the class. Imagine what it's like to walk into a bakery and ask for pecan pie and get a response like, 'what?' and repeating it until I stopped and spelled it instead. Years went by, and I spoke the English language fluently with a large vocabulary and proper grammar, but I still had the accent. When I was a student at Case Western Reserve University, I enrolled in Speech Therapy/Accent Correction at the Cleveland Speech and Hearing Center. I was focused on correcting the 'w,' and 'th,' sounds and which syllable the emphasis belonged on. In Hungarian the emphasis is usually on the first syllable, but in English it is often on the second or third syllable. After a lot of practice, I still had an accent, but it was much improved.

When I finished 8th grade, I was placed into English grammar during summer school before entering high school. As I mentioned before, I studied English grammar in Hungary, and that knowledge suddenly came in very handy. I knew more English grammar than all the American students in my class, who were placed there for various other reasons. When I entered Cleveland Heights High School I was placed into some remedial classes because the administration thought those would be easier for me with limited English. So, I was placed into General Science instead of Biology. This class was a remedial class and the other students had special needs. The teacher quickly realized that I was far ahead of the other students in spite of my limited English and wanted to transfer me into Biology. I liked having an easy class and I begged him to leave me in this class, so he did. In 10th and 11th grades, however, I found myself in Chemistry and Physics. I was no longer in easy classes and I took the SAT for college entrance. By that time my scores were similar to American born English speaking students. I received several scholarships and I ended up in Case Western Reserve University and then at New York University in New York City. While I was at CWRU, in 1968, I became an American citizen, and I could finally say that I am an American!

The immigrant experience was challenging for me, but it was far more difficult for my parents, who were 45 and 53 years old when we arrived.

My mother became involved with private childcare. She loved children, was very creative and liked to do various activities with them. She had several jobs taking care of children for people as she was also picking up the English language. She watched soap operas on TV, read books in Hungarian and some easier books in English. She also started reading the Cleveland Jewish News and the Cleveland Plain Dealer. She copied recipes from the newspaper in English, and she also copied poems into a notebook. She learned to speak English mostly on her own, as she didn't go to school. The process of learning the language was lengthy and problematic at times for both of us. I remember when my mother and I went to the supermarket to buy beans, so she could make cholent (slow baked meat and bean stew). We picked up a bag of what looked like beans to both of us, and we didn't yet understand what was written on the bag. When she attempted to make her cholent she realized that these beans weren't getting soft. They weren't getting soft because they weren't beans; they were some type of nuts. She found this out when she called her sister and read to her what was written on the bag. This became an in-joke and a story that I told many times. She eventually spoke the language fairly well, but her spelling wasn't perfect. Having her sisters and their families around made a huge difference in her life. She spoke to her sisters 2-3 times a day depending on how busy they were, and they could stay on the phone for hours. Our families got together every Saturday and Sunday. They never ran out of things to talk about and never stopped enjoying each other's company.

My father had a more difficult time with finding work and picking up the language, but he succeeded eventually. In Putnok my father owned a shoe store, then became a manager of the shoe store and sold shoes. Then in Budapest he was a Rabbi's Assistant. In Cleveland, when we first arrived, he didn't speak English, so he couldn't work in a shoe store or even in a synagogue at first. The Jewish Family Service found him a job in the maintenance department of the Jewish Community Center in Cleveland Heights as a maintenance man. Before that he also worked in a factory, but that job was too difficult for him, and he had to leave. He stayed at the JCC until he was forced to retire past age 65. As he picked up the English language, he started working part time as a Rabbi's assistant again. He helped in synagogues during the High Holy Days, and joined and led minyans (quorum) at gravesites during burials and stone settings. He used to come home tanned and sunburned from the cemeteries because he spent so much time doing this type of work. Eventually, when my parents moved to an Independent Living Facility for senior citizens my father became the manager of the convenience store in the building which sold groceries and a Rabbi's assistant at the adjoining synagogue. He did this work practically until he had a stroke at age 80. Life in Cleveland was not so easy for my father. He admitted to my mother that he liked the city of Budapest better than Cleveland, but he didn't miss the Communist society. While he got along with all of my mother's family, there was always a bit of competition between the brothers in law regarding how they were each able to make a living. In spite of that the family loved and respected each other and they always enjoyed each other's company. My father enjoyed playing chess with my cousin Vera's young son. My father played for real and didn't hesitate to win; causing the little boy to cry, but learn the hard way. The love and support and presence of the extended family made up for all the challenges that we had to face in Cleveland, and that included my father too.

Both my parents became very proud American citizens shortly after me, five years after they arrived in the United States.

'or the second year, High Holiday services are being conducted at the lusicians's Towers on Lancashire Rd. in the Coventry area for older eople who otherwise would not be able to attend services. Shown here

My father is in the middle: leading High Holy Day Services.

Family and Friends

Family means having someone to love you unconditionally in spite of you and your shortcomings. Family is loving and supporting one another even when it's not easy to do so. Family isn't always about being connected biologically because understands that other things and influences bind us. Family is unrelenting, it's secure and reliable. Family isn't just important; it's what is most important.

Marvin Lazenbury, What Does Family Mean to You

I will never forget the eight years I spent living in Cleveland. Cleveland Heights was one of the Eastern suburbs of Cleveland, and together with University Heights it had a large number of immigrants, many of whom were Jewish Holocaust survivors from Eastern Europe. Little Italy was also part of this area, and it stretched nearly to University Circle where Case Western University, Severance Hall of the Cleveland Orchestra and the Cleveland Historical Society are sitting. In my immediate area we had many Holocaust survivors with their families, first near our apartment building and later near our apartment in a two-family house. We had neighbors from Romania, Hungary, Poland and Israel. In addition, many survivors from my mother's home town, Jolsva (Jelsava), also moved to Cleveland. These women weren't just from her hometown, but they were together in Auschwitz and many of them were at the bomb factory in Allendorf: Elizabeth (Bözsi), Edith, Olga, and later Ica (she was with them in the ghetto and in Auschwitz), Kathy and Juci (Julie). Bözsi was the person who gave my mother hot soup and saved her life in Auschwitz, together with the other prisoners. I feel as if G-d had a plan to bring these survivors together again, so they could share their lives and so that their children could meet. We spent many hours together with my family and with the families of Bözsi, Edith, Olga, Kathy, and Juci as well as with my aunt Ica, uncle Ernő and cousin Eva. We shared holidays, get togethers, simchas, and other occasions, and there was a lot of laughter and talking. These women had a good sense of humor, especially Bözsi and Edith. All these families were at my wedding in October of 1973, are in my wedding pictures and forever in my heart.

I (Livia) am in the center; on the Left my father and my mother; their 25th Anniversary.

From R to L: My mother, my father at his 80th birthday party, cousin Vera and husband.

My cousin Eva joined us in Cleveland in 1969 from Czechoslovakia. She had to stay in Paris while she was waiting for her visa to the United States. When she arrived in Cleveland, she lived with aunt Margo. While in Paris she met her future husband, Jacques, who was also waiting for a visa, but needed to wait longer. Eventually he followed her, but his sister lived in Minneapolis, and that's where he had to go. When they got married Eva followed him to Minneapolis. In the meantime, Eva's parents, Aunt Ica and Uncle Ernő also arrived in Cleveland. My mother now had her two sisters and a brother with her in Cleveland. The extended family grew and became even closer. At one point in time we were all together in Cleveland before some of the family started to disperse.

We, first cousins, Vera, Joe, Ivan, Eva and myself grew very close. Vera was older than the rest of us and had her own family, but we spent time together every week, during holidays and were frequently invited to her lovely house for meals in Beachwood, Ohio. The rest of the cousins spent time together going to the movies or doing other activities. Ivan and I frequently met at events at Case Western Reserve. Eventually we both joined International Folk Dancing at NYU. Ivan stayed in my house in New York for three months. Ivan, Joe, Eva and I are very close in age. Eventually Uncle Irving, Uncle Adolf, and Aunt Zsenka passed away, but my parents, Aunt Margo, Aunt Klara, Vera, Paul and their now four children were still there. However, the cousins stayed connected over time and through the miles and I made frequent visits to Cleveland by myself and then with my husband, Joel and eventually with our children, Erica and Steve. Cleveland became a second home for my children from the time they were born until both my parents passed away; in 1992 (my father) and then in 2008 (my mother).

I have two first cousins in Israel also. My mother's brother, Sanyi and his wife Lili settled in Israel after the war. Sanyi lost his first wife and two little boys in Auschwitz, but he had another daughter with Lili after the war, and her name is Esther (aka Julika). Joel and I visited Sanyi, Lili, Esther, her children and her husband in Ptak Tikva, Israel in 1977. At the same time we visited my father's brother, Hugó, wife, Eva and daughter Rachel (aka Judit) in Bne Brak. We also stayed with Mr. and Mrs. Guttman and met up with their son, Bandika, who was married and had children of his own. My cousin, Esther and I communicate frequently through Email, phone and Facebook. Rachel and I occasionally talk on the phone. Rachel came to New York when I worked in the World Trade Center, and we spent a lot of time together doing sightseeing; she also came to my apartment in Briarwood, where we lived at the time. My uncle Hugó, and aunt Eva also visited New York, where they met my children as well. There was a reunion between my father and Hugó in Cleveland. We have made every effort to stay close with the family who lived far away, and continue to do so with the relatives who are still alive.

I am in the center with Mr. and Mrs. Guttman in Israel.

From L to R Cousin Esther is in the front with her children; the back row: Joel, Avi (Esther's husband), Aunt Lili and Uncle Sanyi (my mother's brother) in Israel

From L to R: Cousin Rachel and me (Livia) in New York.
Uncle Hugó, Aunt Eva, and on top: cousin Rachel and Joel, in Israel.

University

I quickly transitioned from a non-English speaking teenager to a college applicant at Cleveland Heights High School. The Jewish Family Services of Cleveland helped me with this process through testing, gathering my transcript and laying out the options for schools that I was eligible for. I decided to stay in Cleveland, close to my parents and my new found extended family, but I also wanted the experience of campus living, so I enrolled at Case Western Reserve University and lived in the dorms. Many of my friends from high school joined me there. Every two weeks I spent the weekend with my parents and my family. Alternating weekends I stayed on campus with my friends. CWRU was the right fit for me because I was a serious student and it was not a 'party' school. My first roommate was by coincidence also of Hungarian heritage from the West Side of Cleveland. She and I got along well, but she had a lot of emotional issues and eventually dropped out. My second roommate, Lynette was from Harrisburg, Pennsylvania and became a very good friend. She was a nursing student and I studied English and Russian literature, but we went to a lot of events together, and she had an open invitation to my house in Cleveland. She even dated my cousins. My cousin Ivan arranged a double date for us to go to a party, but she ended up marrying the guy who was my date that night; Ivan's friend. Lynette and Henry now live in Philadelphia and we talk, message and visit each other as much as we can.

I graduated CWRU with a teaching degree in English and Russian, but I found out that teaching was not for me. During summers I participated in summer school programs at the University of Toronto and at Indiana University. I loved Toronto and had a very interesting experience in Indiana. My parents also encouraged me to visit cousins in New York, Los Angeles and Toronto. My parents were very supportive of my interests and curiosity. Although my mother wanted me to become a pharmacist, I learned that I didn't like chemistry or physics or advanced math very much, so I didn't follow that route. After my summer travels and lack of career direction I decided to pursue graduate school in Counseling and Guidance. When I visited New York, I spent time with my father's cousins in Brooklyn. They were very hospitable and very accommodating. While I was there, I also visited the Szamet family, who were friends from Putnok and Budapest. Our cousins in Brooklyn also drove me around Manhattan, and I got the feel of the city. New York City seemed like a very exciting place to a young (20 something) Hungarian Jewish American citizen, and I decided I wanted to live there.

I (Livia) am in the center with my friends at
Case Western Reserve University Hillel in the late 1960's.

I applied to New York University and started my Master's program in Counseling and Guidance. Although I was never a party girl, this time I was embracing the Village and all it had to offer. I went to a lot of social events and met many new people. I also wanted to meet someone whom I would be able to share my life with and build a family. Social life became primary, but I was doing well enough in my studies. I also worked part time and then full time at the NYU library. Campus in the Village was hopping and full of life, unlike anything I have ever seen. Some of my other friends from Cleveland Heights High School were there too. In December of 1971 we decided to go to a Chanukah party through the NYU Jewish Club (Hillel) at Loeb Student Center. On December 11, 1971 I met my husband, Joel Rothman, at this Chanukah party. We were married on October 28th of 1973.

New York

Today, New York City is a center for the best financial, legal, technological, medical and scientific minds in the world. It's home to some of the finest educational institutions in the country, such as Columbia University and New York University. And for native New Yorkers, the attraction living here is not just the potential to pass a celebrity on the street or sit near one at a restaurant; it's also realization that New York often reflects the pulse of the nation's intellectual, commercial and financial innovation and discovery.

Donna Palumbo, Why Is New York City One of the Best Places in the World to Live and Work?

I moved to New York City in August of 1971. Life in the City was multifaceted for me. I was a student at NYU, I was living in the Village, and I was working. I started dating Joel four months after I arrived, and our relationship became gradually exclusive. I joined International dancing at NYU with my cousin Ivan, who at the time was a student at Adelphi and frequently came to the Village. I also joined the International Club where I met people from all over the world. I frequented the cafes, restaurants and clubs in the Village. Joel and I had a lot of adventures together after we started dating. As I was finishing my 45 credit Master's program, I found out that New York State changed the requirements for

Counseling and Guidance to 60 credits. This would have meant spending another semester in school. By that time, I was burned out with classes and wanted to move ahead with my life, and finished at NYU with a 45 credit Master's degree.

The Upper East Side

Joel was living with his parents in Cliffside Park, New Jersey, and traveled to and from the City to see me every weekend. Together we decided that he should move into his own apartment and I should move in with him. We found a studio apartment on the Upper East Side which was affordable, and the neighborhood was to our liking. I transferred to a full-time position at the NYU Institute of Fine Arts which was within walking distance to the apartment. I also have to add that we were not yet engaged or married, so I got my own living quarters a few blocks away from him, and shared an apartment with several girls, but I spent most of my time with Joel. The Upper East Side was another fascinating adventure. There were many Hungarian restaurants in the vicinity, which unfortunately are gone now. We frequently ate at 'Tip Top,' where the food reminded me of my mother's cooking. We visited 'Tip Top' frequently even after we moved to Queens. While we were living on the Upper East Side, we realized how much we cared for each other and that we wanted to get married. We became engaged in August of 1973 and celebrated it by going to Mexico, where we had a fantastic vacation.

While I was living in New York City I traveled back and forth to Cleveland to see my family. Eventually Joel came with me, and they welcomed Joel with open arms. Of course, everyone wanted to know when we were getting married. At first, we didn't want to answer those questions, but when we finally got engaged the whole family was ecstatic. My parents arranged and organized our wedding at Davis Caterers in Cleveland Heights, Ohio. We had a beautiful wedding with all of our family and friends. Joel's parents and sister came from New York. It turned out that Joel's father and my mother had something in common and may have crossed paths in the past. Joel's father was in the Army during World War II and was involved in mop up operations in Germany, near Dachau and Buchenwald. This is where my mother was liberated by American soldiers. Many of Joel's friends came to the wedding as well. Cousins from my side came from California, and my Aunt Ica and Uncle Ernő came from Minneapolis. My cousin Vera was my matron of honor and her children were all in the wedding party. Little Mark was to be our ring bearer but he got sick. It was truly a joyous occasion. I married my best friend on October 28th, 1973, on Joel's 32nd birthday, and we celebrated our 48th Anniversary on October 28th, 2021. Our wedding album contains pictures of precious people, and many Holocaust survivors who were truly remarkable and strong.

My Wedding

My wedding in 1973 with Joel, my father and my mother.

From L to R: Joel's sister, Lee, Father, Sam, Livia, Joel, and Joel's mother, Hilda.

From L to R; 1st row: Aunt Klara, Aunt Margo, my mother, cousin Vera, Aunt Ica; 2nd row: cousins: Cheryl, Ivan, Joe, Uncle Adolf, me (Livia), Joel, my father, Paul (Vera's husband), cousin Grace, Uncle Ernő and cousin Steven.

Queens

Queens is the easternmost and largest in area of the five boroughs of New York City, geographically adjacent to the borough of Brooklyn at the western end of Long Island.

www.ny.gov/counties/queens

Living in a studio apartment was challenging. Once we had an argument, so I walked into the bathroom to get some space, but I couldn't come out. The lock broke and I was locked in. We laughed about that many times later, but at the time it was annoying. Joel had to call the maintenance people to get me out of the bathroom. Needless to say we decided to move to a one-bedroom apartment. We loved the Upper East Side and really wanted to stay there. We looked at many apartments in our price range, but couldn't find anything that would be satisfactory. So we did a lot of thinking and decided to look at apartments in Western Queens. Again Forest Hills and other areas closer to the city were too expensive, so we ended up further out, in a fairly spacious one-bedroom apartment in Briarwood. The E and F train subway stops were just a few blocks away and we would commute into Manhattan that way to go to work. We lived in Briarwood until April of 1980.

Career

Even before we started looking at one-bedroom apartments I realized that I needed to change jobs and change careers, so I can earn more money. As I graduated from NYU, I started taking many Civil Service tests for the State, the City and for the Federal Government, and I also became a licensed teacher for New York State. Job offers started coming in. One day I received an inquiry from New York State for Social Security Disability Examiner. The job would be located at World Trade Center #2, and the salary was much higher than what I was getting at the Institute of Fine Arts. I decided to go for the interview, the job was offered to me, and I accepted it. I started working for the New York State Office of Disability Determinations as a Disability Examiner on March 7th, 1974. There were name changes to the office, my position changed due to promotions, and the office moved several times. Thankfully we moved out of the World Trade Center in 1979. I was content with my job and my career with New York State. I also met a lot of new people there, some of whom became my lifelong friends. When my children were born, I was able to take a two year long childcare leave each time. Teaching positions were offered to me very early on after I started this job, but I didn't take them because I knew teaching wasn't for me. My agency opened an office in Queens, so for 18 years I was able to work very close to home, while I was raising my children. After the tragic events of 9/11, when the World

Trade Center was attacked and destroyed with thousands of people in it, my office in Queens closed, and moved back to Downtown Manhattan into the Century 21 building. This building was across the street from the World Trade Center ruins and the construction site of the new buildings. Once again, I became involved in a lengthy commute and the exciting as well as nerve wrecking lower Manhattan experience. Eventually, after working for New York State for 36 years on and off, I retired in 2010.

Fresh Meadows

Fresh Meadows is in Queens County and is one of the best places to live in New York. Living in Fresh Meadows offers residents an urban suburban mix feel....The public schools in Fresh Meadows are above average.

Niche.com/Fresh Meadows - New York City, NY

While we were living in Briarwood, we started talking about making an investment in real estate. We had no idea where we wanted to live or whether we wanted a house, condominium or a co-op. We started looking around in Westchester, Long Island and in Queens. We slowly narrowed it down to Queens, and specifically to School District 26. We had friends who lived in Fresh Meadows, and we decided we liked the area enough to concentrate our efforts there. After looking at many houses we bought the attached town house that we currently still live in 40 years later. We raised our children in this house and they went to District 26 schools. Now it's just the two of us living in this house. Due to the pandemic that started in 2020 we are spending so much more time in the house than we ever thought we would, but this is the place where we now spent most of our marriage, raised our children and spent most of our lives.

Children

We were married in 1973, but we didn't have children until 1981. Some of that wait was voluntary and some of it happened because I had some medical issues and my first pregnancy ended in miscarriage. After all those issues resolved my daughter Erica was born on April 6, 1981; a beautiful baby girl who weighed nearly 9 lbs. Steven, my son, was born on November 8, 1984 with some complications, but all turned out fine. Our family was complete; a boy and a girl, and my life was full. Altogether I used four years of child care leave and also worked part time for a while. We used babysitters while we were both working. I found that raising children is not only the most important, but also the most difficult, challenging and fulfilling job there is.

We had many adventures with the children as they got older and grew into adulthood. The most significant event that ran through their childhood was frequent regular visits to see their maternal grandparents and the extended family in Cleveland. At first, we were there for holidays and vacations, and when the children were in school, we spent school vacations there. Frequently we spent up to two weeks of time there. Also, on the way to Cleveland and back we stopped at vacation spots like Hershey Park, the Poconos, the Football Hall of Fame in Canton, Ohio, the Catskills, Cedar Point Amusement Park. During our stay in Cleveland we always spent time with Aunt Margo, Aunt Klara, Vera, Paul, and their children and grandchildren if they were in town. We took the children to Cleveland 2-3 times a year from the time they were born until they became adults. When they got older, they went to Cleveland on their own to visit my mother and any other family who was still there, like my cousin Vera. My father passed away in 1992, and we still made multiple trips to my mother every year until she passed away in 2008. Even since 2008 we all took a trip to Cleveland to the unveiling of my mother's grave stone. During the summer of 2020 we were scheduled to visit my parents' graves as well as my cousin Vera and her daughter Grace. Because of the COVID-19 pandemic we had to cancel the trip. Also unfortunately and very unexpectedly my cousin Vera passed away at age 84. We still plan to travel to Cleveland again at the end of this pandemic to visit the cemetery and to see cousin Grace.

My parents' decision to leave Hungary shaped my life. It was because of that move that I became part of a large and loving extended family. Also the move to the United States provided me with options that I never would have had in Communist Hungary. I live in a Democracy where

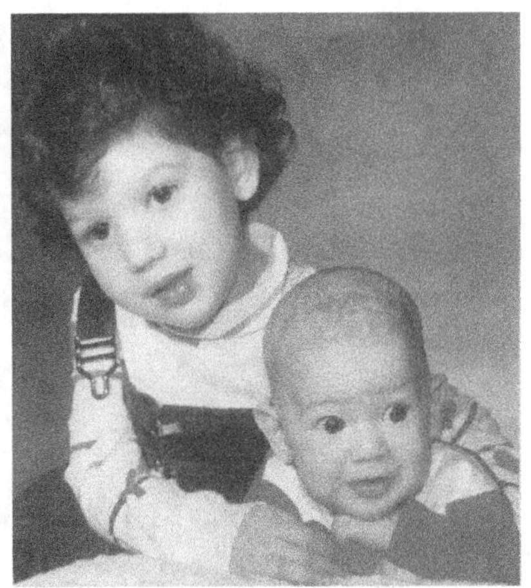

My children: Erica and Steven.

My mother and father with Joel, Erica and Steve in Cleveland.

From L to R: on top: my mother, me (Livia), Aunt Margo, Aunt Klara, and my children on the bottom, in Cleveland.

Joel and I with Erica and Steve, vacationing at Hershey Park; on our way to Cleveland.

Erica with my mother (age 90) at the nursing home in Cleveland in 2008. This is the last picture I have of my mother before she passed away in November of 2008. Erica and Jason visited my mother together in July of 2008.

we have freedom of speech, freedom of religion, freedom of the press and many other freedoms that nobody should ever take for granted. We also have more than one political party, and we vote for our government representatives every year. In some ways because of this freedom life is more complicated. People don't hesitate to express and act on their political views and differences. People also gather to demonstrate, riot, and complain about issues that they find unfair. Unfortunately this often can turn into physical violence, and because of the right to carry weapons gun violence has always been evident. For the sake of our children, grandchildren and other descendants I hope that we will continue to live in a free and Democratic society with more control on crime and violence. I say 'Never Again' to another Holocaust and any other genocides! All human beings of all colors, sexual preference, all religions and all genders deserve to live free and free of prejudice, discrimination and violence. And I say thank you to my parents for facing many challenges and bringing me to a free country with a lot of opportunities, introducing me to an amazing family and giving me an opportunity to raise my children here.

Epilogue

As I reflect on my life, although it has had many challenges, I have had a good life so far. I am sure that I will have more challenges, but I will continue to love and enjoy my family and friends, and participate in events and activities that I like.

What I learned from my parents, their experiences and the way they lived their lives is that no matter what happens people always have options in how to react. When an event occurs in life each person has to evaluate those options available to him/her and decide which option to take. I have heard many times, in response to the atrocities of the Holocaust, 'why did people not fight back.' People in fact did react in ways they were equipped to react. Considering that firearms were illegal and not available they could not physically fight, but they used many other options. Some people found a way to escape, some felt that an attempted escape was too dangerous and risky. Some, like my aunts and uncles, decided to hide in the forests and mountains, but that came with its own consequences. My Aunt Klara and her husband felt their young children wouldn't survive the conditions, so they sent their children to a safer environment. They made a decision that they could live with at the time, which they were sure was the best decision for their children. There was no way of predicting that two years later those children would no longer be safe in their surroundings. Even with those disastrous consequences of their decision they found a way to live and rebuild their lives. The philosophy behind this is that people always have to make the best decision for themselves, and the best decision is always the one that you can comfortably live with. When you are faced with the consequences of that decision, again you have to find a way to live with those consequences.

I learned through my family's experiences as well as through my own, that life is constantly full of obstacles, but I learned to be flexible and taught my children to be flexible.

My parents taught me, by example, to make a life for myself that I can be content with. They faced challenges and became stronger. They survived the Holocaust and rebuilt their lives. I was born, and they raised me with love and sacrifices. We moved around in search of a better life and we found it. With this life story I am passing this legacy to my children, grandchildren and all future descendants. Live your best life, examine your options, make decisions that you can comfortably live with and then find a way to live with the consequences in a way that you can be content!

Joel and I still live in our house in Fresh Meadows, Queens, New York. We try to see our friends and family as much as possible during the current COVID-19 pandemic, mostly outside under safe conditions. At this time we are hoping for this pandemic to come to an end as soon as possible and to resume normal activities and travel.

Our daughter, Erica lives on Long Island with her husband, Jason, and two children. Our grandson and granddaughter are the loves of our lives. Erica has a Bachelor's degree in Early Childhood Education and many years of experience working with children.

Our son, Steve lives in Forest Hills, Queens and works as an LMSW (Social Worker).

My cousin Eva lives in Minneapolis with her husband, three children and six grandchildren.

My cousin Joe lives in Omaha, Nebraska.

My cousin Ivan lives in Cranston, Rhode Island with his wife. He has two sons.

Grace, Vera's daughter, lives in Cleveland with her husband.

Cheryl, Vera's younger daughter lives in Virginia with her daughter.

Steve, Vera's son lives in California with his wife. He has three daughters and had one son (deceased), who was Vera's first grandchild.

Mark, Vera's younger son lives in Virginia with his wife and has three children and one grandchild.

I have two cousins who live in Israel:

Esther, Sanyi's (my mother's brother) daughter lives in Petak Tikvah and has three children, and eight grandchildren.

Rachel, Hugó's daughter lives in Bne Brak with her husband, three children and four grandchildren.

In spite of the too many family members that were murdered during the Holocaust we have many descendants and will continue to have more. This is the best revenge!

Legacy

From L to R: Livia, Erica, Jason, Steve, Joel, Erica and Jason's children (our grandchildren).

Family Photos

My maternal grandmother, Ethel.

My maternal grandfather, Eugene (Jeno).

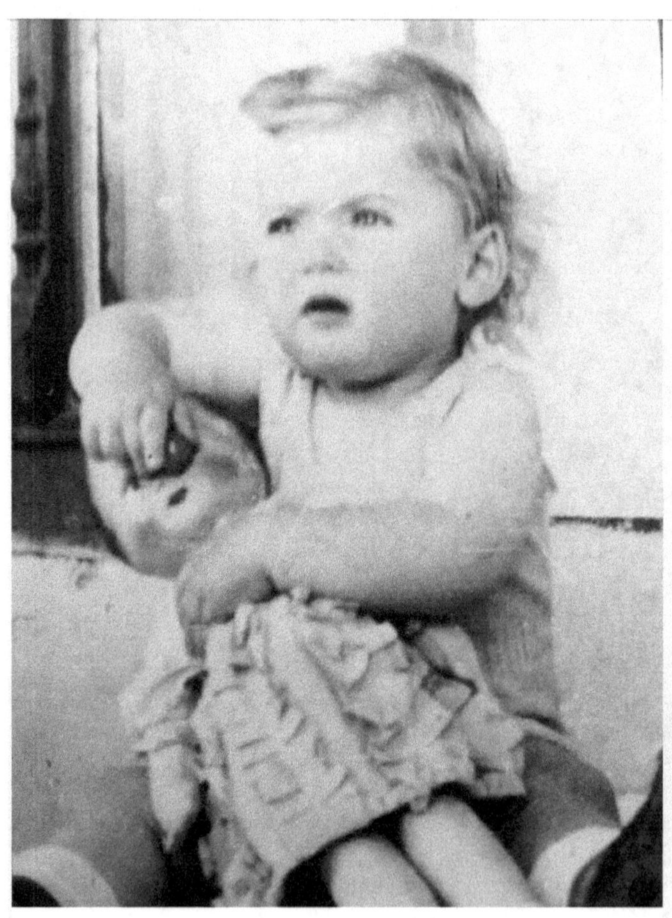

Marika, Ernő's daughter.

Aunt Klara's children: on top: Vera, on the bottom: Adi.

My Uncle Sanyi's wife, Elza, and children, Robi and Tomi. He survived Forced Labor.

ALSO MURDERED IN AUSCHWITZ:
Irén Kaufmann, Marika's mother
My paternal grandfather, Henrik Birnbaum
(My paternal grandmother, Regina Birnbaum, died before World War II).
My father's sister, Elza Birnbaum and her family

My Uncle Edmund (my mother's brother) was murdered in
Hungarian Forced Labor at the Russian Front.

From L to R: Joel, Steve, Erica, and Livia.

From L to R: My mother (Vali), Aunt Klara, Uncle Ernő, Aunt Margo.

From L to R: My mother (Vali), Aunt Klara, cousin Ivan, Aunt Margo, cousin Vera, Vera's husband Paul, Uncle Ernő, Aunt Ica, Joel's mother Hilda, Steve.

From L to R: Rabbi, Erica, Steve, Joel and Livia.

From L to R: in front: Livia, Steve, Joel; in back: Hilda, cousin Ivan, Erica, my mother (Vali)

Erica and Jason, September 6, 2009.

L to R: Joel, Erica, Jason, Livia, Steve.

From L to R: Cousin Vera, Joel's cousin Paul and wife Zelda, Joel, Livia, Erica, Jason, Joel's sister Lee, Steve, cousin Eva, husband Jacques and cousin Joe.

Erica, Jason and their children (our grandchildren).

Bibliography

Kramer, John M. "Drug Abuse in Eastern Europe: An Emerging Issue of Public Policy." https//www.jstor.org/stable/2500413. Slavic Review, vol. 49, no. 1, 1990, pp. 19-31. JSTOR, Accessed 5 Dec. 2020.

Nebiolo, Molly. "Mental Health under the Hungarian People's Republic." Guestwriter. https://medicalhealthhumanities.com. Accessed 5 Dec. 2020.

Kellerman, Natan. "The long-term psychological effects and treatment of Holocaust trauma." https://wwwresearchgate.net. Journal of Loss and Trauma, 6(3):197-218. Accessed 5 Dec.2020.

Gaal, Peter. S. Zigeti. M. Csere. M. Gaskins. D. Panteli. Health Systems in Transition. Vol.13 No 5 2011. Hungary. Health System Review. https://www.euro.who.int/. European Observatory on Health Systems and Politics. Accessed 5 Dec. 2020.

Molnar, Laszlo. "Anti-Semitism in Hungary." No.104. https://jcpa.org/article/anti-semitism. Accessed 5 Dec. 2020.

Helmreich, William B. Against All Odds: Holocaust Survivors and the Successful Lives They Made in America (Library of Conservative Thought). 2nd edition.

United States Holocaust Memorial Museum. Holocaust Encyclopedia. "Death Marches." https://encyclopedia.ushmm.org. Accessed 5 Dec. 2020.

Yad Vashem. Articles. "Liberation and the Return to Life. The First Moments of Liberation." https://www.yadvashem.org/. Accessed 5 Dec 2020.

United States Holocaust Memorial Museum. Holocaust Survivors and Victims Database. Files Related to 17000 Forced Laborers Who Worked in Munition Factories in Stadtallendorf. (ID:30511). https://www.ushmm.org/online. Accessed 5 Dec 2020.

Grace, Michael L., Posted June 3, 2011. "History of the Italian Line and the MS Vulcania. https://www.cruiselinehistory. Accessed 5 Dec. 2020.

Llewellyn, Jennifer. S, Thompson. "Janos Kadar." Alpha History. October 30, 2018. https://alphahistory.com/coldwar/janos-kadar. Accessed 5 Dec. 2020.

Stark, Tamas. Antisemitic Writings of the Arrow Cross Emigration. Chapter 9. https://link.springer.com/chapter/. Accessed 5 Dec. 2020.

The Holocaust Chronicle. 1942: The "Final Solution." "Munkaszolgalat." 2009 Publications International, Ltd. http://www. holocaust chronicle.org/.staticpages/324.html.Accessed 5 Dec. 2020.

Weissman, Rabbi. "Rabbi Announces Deportation of Hungarian
     Jewry." Jewish Virtual Library, A Project of AICE. https://www.
     jewishvirtuallibrary.org/. Accessed 5 Dec. 2020.

Yad Vashem. "Murder of Hungarian Jewry." https://www.yadvashem.org/.
     holocaust/about/fate-of-jews/.hungary.html. Accessed 8
     Dec. 2020.

Haraszti, Gyorgy. Translated by Veronika Szabo. "Hungary. Hungarian
     Anti-Jewish Legislation, 1938-1944." Jewish Social Studies vol. 48,
     no. 1, 1986, pp. 63-82. JSTOR, www.jstor.org/stable/4467318.
     Accessed 8 Dec. 2020.

Braham, Randolph L. The Destruction of Hungarian Jewry: A Documentary
     Account In two volumes. New York: Pro Arte for the World
     Federation of Hungarian Jews. 1963. Pp. cxxxvi, 416; 417-969.

Dokumentation der Internationalen Tage der Begegnung In
     Stadtallendorf. KZ-Aufenlager Munchmule/Nobel. Vom 21.bis
     26.10.1990. 1991 by Magistrat der Stadt Stadtallendorf und
     Forderverein fur Stadt- und Regionalgeschichte Stadtallendorfs
     1933-1945 e.V.

Radnóti, Miklós. The Complete Poetry in Hungarian and English.
     McFarland & Company, Inc., Jefferson, North Carolina.

Palumbo, Donna. Why Is New York City One of the Best Places in the World
     to Live and Work? https://www.worth.com/advice. Accessed
     31 Dec. 2020.

Hernandez, Araceli. What Every American Should Know About the Immigrant Experience. https://www.aspeninstitute.org/blog-posts/. Accessed 31 Dec. 2020.

Reiber, Beth. 10 Things You Might Not Know About Cleveland, Ohio. Dec. 27, 2019. USA Today/10 Best Features. Thisiscleveland.com. Accessed Dec. 31, 2020.

Peter, Laszlo. Budapest, national capital, Hungary. https://www.brittanica.com/place/Budapest. Accessed Dec 31, 2020.

Brown, Eva with Thomas Field-Meyer. If You Save One Life, A Survivor's Memoir. The Upper Story Press, Los Angeles, California. 2007.

Lazenbury, Marvin. MHS. What Does Family Mean to You. https://www.beststrongfamilies.org/news/2018/9/28/

https://www.ny,gov/counties/queens. Accessed 1 January 2021.

https://www.niche.com/places-to-live/n/fresh-meadows-new-york-city-ny/ Accessed 1 January 2021.